AF265587

A NEW ROOT

by

Joy Waring

A NEW ROOT

Joy Waring

Unless otherwise indicated, all Scripture quotations are taken from the New King James Version of the Bible (NKJV)

A New Root

ISBN 978-0692944134

Copyright © 2017 by Joy Waring

Printed in the United States of America. All rights reserved under International Copyright Law. Contents and/or cover may not be reproduced in whole or in part in any form without the express written consent of the Author.

DEDICATION

I want to dedicate my first book of poetic writings to those who have truly inspired my freedom from within.

To "A Sweet Little Star," my daughter Jada thank you for *seeing me.* To my parents Sharon, Darrell and Sharee, your love for me is uncompromising. To my sister Faith thank you for walking with me through this poetic journey. To my grand mother Caroline without you where would we be and my dear friend, Mrs. Temple; thank you all, you will never be forgotten.

A special thanks to my Pastors, Dr. Dexter and Lady Leisa Easley for your 'stand'. I love you both. And special thanks to Christopher Reynolds and Venice Eaddie.

Each of you have been a strong support and encouraged me at all points of need in my life, fostering the gifts within me.

CONTENTS

DEDICATED TO YOU

'The Lord your God has multiplied you, and here you are today, as the stars of heaven in multitude.
[11]'May the Lord God of your fathers make you a thousand times more numerous than you are, and bless you as He has promised you!

Deuteronomy 1:10-11

The Lord has been mindful of us; He will bless us; He will bless the house of Israel; He will bless the house of
Aaron. [13]He will bless those who fear the Lord, both
small and great. [14]May the Lord give you increase more
and more, you and your children. [15]May you be blessed
by the Lord, who made heaven and earth.

Psalms 115:12-15

Never Alone

They laughed and said
"Look, what is she doing, she's weird"
"Why is she the only one standing there?"

Hands lifted.
They called me a loner.

I was the only one they saw.
Because I am the only one
that's free

I'm not offended.
Even the tree stood there
beside me
with its arms stretched out like me,
Like Me.

Battle With Me

I thought the only battle
I would have is with the enemy.

And I planned to fight
with every inch of me.
And when I won, I sat down
So I could breathe.

And when I looked up
I couldn't believe
I saw myself standing in front of me.

I wanted war with myself.
I was my enemy.

I don't create my own power
so I won't bow before my shadow.

I declare and decree
that my *free will* won't capture me.

Better Than This

When I see myself
detouring from the route
the Lord has set for me;
my thoughts
will come out and stand in front of me
and say, "You're better than this"

When I begin to challenge
the purpose the Lord has given me;
set myself up for limitations,
instead of seeking out my Creator;
my thoughts will tap my heart and say,
"Lay heavy, she's better than this"

When I find myself frustrated
my thoughts will partner with my heart
and they'll party on my sleep time,
deprive me of my rest until I realize,
I'm better than this.

Our Bond Time

If the world shows its tongue to me
or mouths find the time to curse me,
I'll never let the moment
scorn the value of our bond time.

When eyes begin to stalk me
or the clouds turn gray
and spit on me,
I'll never let the disrespect
party on our bond time.

Even when the flowers bloom
and everyday the sun shines on me.

I'll never let the pleasant life
set aside our bond time.

There She Is

Everywhere she went, I was there.
I watch her every morning;
wash her face, she kisses her kids;
she does everything she can
to keep her spirit awake.
Out there on the field,
Planting seeds in the garden.

And as I watch her,
my eyes by passed her clothing
and she became transparent.
Then I saw her speaking spirit
and how her heart is fixed on Him.

I noticed the shape of her wings
and her ability to move it through the wind.
She doesn't stay still for too long
so please don't be offended.
She's just on a different path
and desires His perfect will.

They ask her,
What makes your fruit so sweet?
How do you maintain this view?
And she replies,
"I uproot everything of unredeeming value"

How increase and prosperity
sits in her mouth
like taste buds on her tongue.

She has so much wisdom
you would think Proverbs birthed her.
She mindfully guards the gateways
to her spirit.
Her meditation is upright
so her inner image is greatness.

Her 'I AM's buckle her
and keeps her safe.
Then she saw me watching,
she smiled, I chuckled.
I knew her actions,
but I was just too busy to honor her face.

Right then my eyes began to rain
when I realized she was me.
I am a Woman.

Living The Life

I want to live the life
of waking up to say,
'I'm happy'
because of my yesterday,

My own kind try to poke me
with their own vaccine;
to provide immunity
against my own destiny.

But my casket
won't hold
no one but me.

They're mad.
Well, I'll let them be
because this life;
my life
was given to me.

I am the 'get away'
in this generation.

And I will live my life here -
up until my graduation.

The Best Days

I have a great life.
I'm living in my best days
with a shout a little louder
and it all goes to my Father.
I am the walking proof of God's grace.

I have a great life.
I'm living in my best days.
This is a poem and a song
I will praise the name of Yah.

I know you see the look on my face.

I have a great life.
I'm living in my best days.
If it had not been for You,
I'd be trudging through the day
just a body on its way.

Thank You Lord.
Now I am living.

A Reminder

You kept reminding me
in the middle of my stray,
my life is not my own.
Your love is here to stay.

I'm alive with You
that is why I feel this way.

I've seen roads
You haven't set for me to take.
And I refused,
because I refuse to walk the route
that decorates my grave.

I will not party with the enemy
or dance upon the death of me.
I'm here to live for You.
For me to live again.

A Shift

I took one look and started running.
Something seeped inside of me
that was more important
than the ground under me.
I ran right off the cliff
but death didn't capture me.
His presence held onto me.

Never thought I could fly
but there I was above the clouds
going up at a high rate of speed.

I am the One,
'The Getaway'
and in my hand I hold the key.

The world waited for me to peek back,
to mourn and miss the disguised life.
But flesh, I will not cry for you
with a bittersweet goodbye.

Breaking Free

As Your hands stretched for me,
I met You at the altar,
received a gift; then tongues.

Right then I felt the tug.
The tug of death for the world.
The tug of strength for life.

The difference between existing
versus I'm really alive.
And when I joined with You
I was no longer blind.
My eyes were then unveiled.
The shadow then left behind.
Unconsciously unraveled
the knots that tied me down.

I shouted with lifted hands.
"I'm free from limitations.
I'm no longer astray from life!"

I realized I reached freedom
when my limit,
was no longer the sky.

I am renewed, much better than before
with my foot on the devils neck,
I spread my wings to soar.

The Prodigal

I saw the curse
and I fell into the dark hole
that offered me what I asked for.

But I realized with everything in front of me,
I was losing without Him.
The enemy thought he had me
but he misjudged.
He didn't see a fight in me
but that didn't make me vulnerable.

He saw the building coming down.
but missed the foundation it stood on.
He trembled.
He knew that familiar strength to my walk
and this time; breast plate and all -
armored up.

I won't settle again.
It is I that made the mistake
but it was him that had mistaken me.

I am The Prodigal
covered by grace and mercy.

All For You

If the world offers me
what I ask for,
I will still call on Your name.
I will still submit to You.

Once my fridge is full
and I can share my goods with nations
I will still sit at Your table.
I will still call You able
because without You;
with money, I'd still be poor.
With food, I'd still be hungry.
A healthy body, yet still sick,
because it is You
who breathes life into me for my tomorrow.

Why would I let
the perfect life
set aside my bible?

My Life On You

I'm still excited.
Since the day I laid my life on You.
I told my heart and mind
they have to follow suit.
Then a song started inside my chest.
My heart beating the drum.
My thoughts are dancing to it.

Since I chose You,
my life now has its own music.

Oh, I'm so glad
my life has been renewed
and I'm thankful
because I laid my life on You.

Saved From Sin

I remember
right in the party of sin,
I felt Your tug,
Your gripping love.
And even though
I stepped back,
You stayed one step ahead
just a reach away.

My eyes were enlightened
to what I called fun.

Sin with a smile
Looked at me
And dropped down to its feet.
with a knife behind
its back begging for me.

Thank You Lord
You saved me.

Victor

I won't repeat my past;
a life that I once cancelled.
A mountain I tried to climb,
destroying it was better.

And every door I pass
I destroy the key.

As a Victor,
I'm not a victim
to peek back on a defeat.

You may not know me well
but mouths have told my story.

Once again, I'm not a victim.
I've won and now victorious.

You may try to rewind me
to what I've torn asunder.
But then I'll remind you
that I am an overcomer.

Jump Into The Unclear

This is what I know
but I know this isn't it.
I can no longer linger here
so I'm on the run from it.

This tradition twins with religion.
I know, this is not Your will.
Rules? Trade off?
You do? I do?
There's just one way out.
To risk it…

I admit, this step is unclear.
And I'm one step behind this cliff.
So then I jump the jump of faith.
Nothings under, but I'm not falling.

Right then I knew,
I'm onto my next dimension
carried by my Father.

Remembering You

I remember you said,
'I am the head and not the tail'
and You said
'You'll make an everlasting covenant
with me if I incline my ear.'

You also said,
No good is withheld from me,
Your blood is armor to me.

It's what You said.

I'm just remembering what You said.

I won't let pressure hinder my praise.
I still have faith
from my remembering days.

Deuteronomy 28:13
Psalms 84:11
Isaiah 55:3

BULLIES

They got mad
and cursed me.
Shouted my name
and wronged me.
They don't know who I am.

I don't place a mask
at my bedside.
I won't lose myself in them.
I won't become a puppet
to those puppeteers.

They're trying to get my attention
but I won't even quench their thirst.
So they got mad and cursed me,
shouted my name and wronged me.

Just Us

They mocked me as I sang
to our sweet song.
You're more important than they
so I keep singing along.

I love the way You make me feel.

They laughed as I danced,
and pulled the rug from under me.
But they won't interrupt my sway
to our sweet song.
One day they'll wish
they danced along.
This is our moment.

I love the way You make me feel.

They tell me I was persuaded,
by a sinful man.
You are who I believe You are
and they don't understand,
I sold myself to You,
because of the way You make me feel.

Unlike Them

They called out to me
but I didn't come.
I'm unlike them.

If I come out of His will
a thick cloud would hit earth
and fog my vision.

Then I'd be a follower.
I have to take a route
That keeps me under His umbrella.

They kept calling out to me
but I didn't come.
The calling from my Father
is too strong.

They told me other successful plans;
most of them were right,
but those won't work for me.
My Father perfects my life.

I wasn't saddened -
- this isn't something I'd escape from.

They won't stop.
They keep calling,
waiting for me to come
but I won't -
I'm unlike them.

Tuned Out

They called me cocky,
I closed my ears
because I don't want to hear it.

They're doubting the Great God.
Why would I listen to them?
Pass me the cotton, turn up the music.
Anything to block out the dead.

"There she is, her cocky self. With her ears
covered. Don't bother, she won't listen."

I laugh at them.
If they asked me why,
I'll gladly tell them,
it's my thankfulness that keeps me.

I shout because I understand;
if it had not been for Jesus,
I would've died
in the same sin
I was in...
with them.

To My Enemies

I hear that you can't hold your tongue
from speaking against me.

I hear that you won't seal your lips
from words of negativity.

Here is my prayer for you:

Lord forgive them.
Open their eyes to see truth.
I know they hate me
because my decision is not a debate.
Please don't let their mouths
be a shovel for their graves.

Let Your love never leave my face.
I hope they watch me so much
till one day they will be saved.

My Passing Places

I don't want to remember you-
my passing places.
You've passed away and buried deep.
That's the reason you can't bother me.
I vow to never give you attention
which makes it easy to ignore you.
I will not visit you, like a candle lit memorial.

Beyond

I'm beyond
what the world thinks of me.

Beyond a statistic.

Beyond the gossiping tongues
with eyes that see a branch of me.

I'm beyond being offended.
I'm deaf to negativity.

Since those remarks aren't beyond me.

Hi
Naïve is what they call me
since I go to sleep stress free,
knowing everyone loves me.

His Soldier

I pray for my enemies
and buy food for those
who may starve me.

I'm His Soldier!

Do you see me coming?
Fully armored and all.
Don't tremble,
I won't rise in pride over your downfall.

I have a good prayer for you.

I'm His Soldier!

I won't party in your trouble,
that's not a victory for me
even I do not deserve,
but My God still gives to me.

I'm His Soldier!

My Place

This is the place my praise arises.
The place I come to,
my inner circle.
This is the place no one can follow.
Only He has access to it.

This is the place where I draw closer
into the heart where love dwells.

This is the place they ask,
"Where is it?"

But this place,
I won't tell.

This is the place,
a place of peace.

This is my secret place.

Out Of This World

Out of this world
I'm gone…
to the place in my heart
I belong.

Believe it or not
I'm there
What's done in Heaven
Shall be done here.

I'm not of this world
nor captured
so I don't take offense
to its offers.

I'm out of this world but I'm still in it.
You have to be out of this world,
just to get it.
I've gained weight and now I don't fit in it.

Born unto Him,
A birth over again.

I'm sold out of this world
I'm Gone.

Enjoying Nature

I hear the ocean, the wind,
and the trees as they speak.
For a second, I saw nature
as a worship team

I gaze at the trees,
and how their branches are raised.
I'm so full by the sight,
of nature giving You praise.

Your nature is in me,
That's why I feel this way.

I love how the wind
tickles a tune in my ear.
You placed me here.
So I'm enjoying this view.
Me, the sightseer
who's passing through.

I'm so amazed at Your hands
and how You drew out this world.
And as I daze into it
I feel my lips curl.

His Love

Because of His love
I have liberty, I have freedom.

He rose so I can rise too
and be forgiven.

I've been washed, now cleansed
because He died for me
and now He lives in me.

His love stretches out like arms
that will hug me while I weep.

His love, loves me.

Entertaining Great Thoughts

I pulled up
me, the passenger
with a daze and a smile.
I can't believe it.
My dream car
parked at her house.
I walked inside,
went up the stairs,
turned the knob to my mansion
and laid down on my king size bed.
And then the thought struck again;
so I got up and ran to the window
to get the best view
of my imagination.
There it was, so shiny and brand new.
I just love
the eyes I see through.
I didn't tell a soul,
they may think I'm insane.
I stepped into persuasive faith
and became -
the thought,
I entertained.

Gods' Timing

I almost gave up
until I heard the sweetest sound.
My greatest time approached me
with my head down.
I thought time was wasted until
I heard His clock tick.

Doesn't it amaze you?
It's a melody to me.
I love to move to the song
that His clock sings.
I heard the buzzer.
I wasn't there
and someone yelled to me
"You're Finished"
But, I'm moved by the song
that His clock sings.

Moments

I am His
so I can't get knocked down.
I stand with His strength
so I can not be shaken
because I'm His.
I received life with His promises;
that makes me moments away
to prosperity -
to all of my dreams.
I close my eyes and still see
what is suppose to be.
Just my visions
of life at its best.
Now I'm in route with my faith.
I'm just a moment to it.

Made Special

Do you know how special I am?
Or the way my heart is conditioned?
How my words are like judges
that brings an order to existence?
I am ordained to triumph;
that means impossible to lose.
So if I seek a threshing floor
then let my gift stir
while I'm in the midst of this snooze.

Supernatural Occurrences

Still like the finish line

and blessings race towards me

coming from unexpected places

and unexplained sources.

Eyes

Eyes you must fix yourself.

I've worn my glasses

as if it was needing to my outfit.

Get in place.

I'm promised you will open,

I'm convinced,

a report will show you perfect.

To My Greatest Pain

I would never settle for you,

Oh my greatest pain.

Don't you know that I am greater?

I'm most valuable to Him.

If you don't understand,

listen, then let it brew.

I will accomplish everything

I said I would do.

Health

Body you must line up with my purpose.

Lord you said that I am healed

Thank you for bringing health to me.

Let the doctors call me different.

I don't follow the statistics.

Because I know without a doubt,

I'm worth more than this.

So, I'll step back and let you

glorify your name in this.

Pressure

Pressure, do you know

what I have packed in me?

I'll have you know

I will explode with power instantly.

You may sneak me with no warning

like a snake strikes

but even out of my mutter

comes His word of life.

My Smile

I smile because this is my season
and every time I smile
my smile has a reason.

My smile will last forever,
I'll smile for eternity.

A smile that looks better
when it smiles back at me.

Hey? Do you notice my smile from a far?
How it justifies its meaning
and shines like the evening star?

My smile, my personal friend.
I'm overwhelmed with happiness;
it's showing out from within.

I smile, because I have Him in me
and if I were to cry
my crying smile would be worth framing.

My Step

I’ve got this step
that doesn't step the same.

The step that’s dressed with favor
every step after is greater.

If I step to a defeat
that’s just a step to conquer
to glorify my Father.
A step of the overcomer
A step of integrity
A step that stays prepared
A step that doesn't leave
unless the next step is cleared.

Like day, my step arises
and praise is my strength.

Lord keep me in your path,
orchestrate my steps.

The Glory

I don't wonder why they stare
because it amazes me.

Even I sit back
and contemplate the Glory over me.
My stand is solid,
I won't slip,
and neither will my dream.

It made them snicker
when they saw me on my knees.

Now those locked jaws are confused
because my smile came out of me.

But truly it's not a mystery,
it's just the Glory over me.

The Scent

I act on this scent -
the scent that hugs my nose,
the scent that lingers over me
and bounces off my clothes.

I watched them point me out.
"I saw her, there goes the giver"
One asked "How did you know?"
"By the way my nose quivered."

They said "I know your scent,
you couldn't hide it if you tried."
I told them "Yes, I know,
because it glows when I pass by."

I love this scent,
the scent that hugs my nose.
The scent that lingers over me
and bounces off my clothes.

The Scent
Part II

I remember the scent.
The scent that hugs my nose.
The scent that lingers over me
and bounces off my clothes.

The scent that prevents
lack from knocking at my door.
Eyes following me.
I'm as amazed as you are
at the beauty of my décor.

I get a whiff of my scent
when I forget it's on me.
It reminds me of His promise;
'give and it'll come back to me.'

I remember the scent.
The scent that hugs their noses.
This scent is the reservoir
to the beauty of my décor.

Peace On Earth

Here I am now
laid back with pretzel legs,
ears being soaked by the stream
coming from my face.

I'm in love with you;
that is why I feel this way.

They witness my shimmer,
even I can see the gleam.

I'm in a daze.
I never thought I'd see the days on earth
when peace proposed to me.

Back To The Wall

Here I am back to the wall again,
with my back to the wall again.
Head tilted and smiling.

Don't think I am in trouble.
This is one of my happy moments
when struggle put its hand on me
and push me to the wall.

I wonder who gave it the nerve
to try and stunt my growth,
to keep me on the growth curve.

Ha, it makes me chuckle
when my back is to the wall again
because when I mark the top of my head
I realize every time, I'm still

Growing.

Cast My Cares

I refuse to worry

because worry defeats my prayer.

I will not waste the wisp of vapor that I am

like I have set aside a spare;

so I humble myself under His mighty hand.

The Praise I Have For You

The kind of praise
I have inside;
if I shout
I'll shock myself.

The kind of praise
that can't be hidden.
Lord knows when I tuck it in, it tickles my insides.

It's not the right place to scream
so I hold it with a smile.
They're watching me
tap my feet.

They see the worship in my eyes.
Oh, I can't hold it,

If I exhale
every angel in Heaven will rise.
Glory to God.
I'm so full,
it's the praise I have inside.

I Must Go

If I have all or nothing
and He speaks
I must go without a question
ready or unprepared
I must leave without an answer.

He said "Go"
I must leave
He made me custom to change
and If I stay,
I'll lose myself in trying to maintain.

I've died to myself.
I'm in Him, and He's in me,
so its painful to remain the same.

He said "Go"
I may have to leave without a sound
So I won't be hindered with
"Please stay here;"
or people comparing
my priorities with theirs.
He said "Go"
I must leave. If I stay, it's my fault.

I don’t want to wonder in a few years
and ask myself, "Where did I go wrong?"
I won’t let disobedience
become my default.

So when He says "Go,"
I must leave don't get comfortable with me.

When He says "Go,"
I must leave.
He is important to me.

My Journey

You told me to go
and it took me long to get there.
But I went and all I see is dry land.

I'm here.
"Stress! Lean up and get off of me!"

Lord, open up my ears
so I can hear Your plans clear.
Enlighten my eyes,
so I can see what You see.

I'm going out in a praise.
This is my blessing.
Let my faith magnify the steps
You placed in front me.
I give it all to You.
Take control of me.

No hindrance shall come
to lock away my dream.

I bound all things
trying to hold all good from me.

Keep me in Your path.
I want what You have for me.

I see wealth come up the street;
it's looking at me.
I'm smiling because I made it.

And I'm smiling because I'm thankful.

Pride, stand aside, I need to stay humble
and if I turn, make me uncomfortable.

I don't want the worlds glitter
to hypnotize me.

Transition

I love to be in Your presence.
Will You make me Your piano
and play Your heart out with me?

You're the best to me.
When I'm with You,
Your love for me and mines for You
creates its own tune.

That's when people find the time
To ask me, What's wrong?
Nothing.
I'm in transition, I may be quiet
but I promise I'm just fine.

You're dealing with me.
I wish they let me finish my session.

They watch my action
and base my results.
But sometimes my actions
are an understatement
to my response.

I can't help it.
Don't think I'm nonchalant.
I know my life itself is a blessing,
but sometimes my flesh
can't properly compliment my spirits expression.

Please, don't be offended
if my appearance didn't shout
like you expected.

I'm being filled with greatness.
And while I'm in the process,
I won't match my animation.

The World To Me

This world reminds me of all it's trying to do
to take me away from You.
Paint a bigger picture,
but it's showing itself confused
because there is only one bigger
and my focus remains on You.

This world isn't meant for me but I expect
it to work out in my favor.
Even if the world rumbles
and sends a wave under my feet,
I hope it drops me to my knees
so my spirit will rise in me
to remind me of this weakling
I sacrificed and died once too,
so it won't take over and capture me.

You're the only one I'll submit too.

The sky is covered,
the clouds are dark,
but I see the way piercing through.

My walk is straight.
I'll remain in peace as long as my eyes
remain on You.

WEALTHY

They tried to shame me
because they saw me
wealthy with my hand out?

They're ignorant to Your word
Lord. They don't know my prayer.
They called me greedy
but I don't care.
They're confused
because I happily bow my head
before You,
hungry, yet I'm full.

They don't get it,
They say
"You shout that you're so rich,
Why must you ask for more"?

To overflow.

My prayer is, they begin to understand my source
instead of try to foil my growth.
I checked Your will.

To be unclothed is not what You have for me.
So, here's my hand Lord,
place in me prosperity
so I can be a two edged sword.

In expression of gratitude to those who have inspired me and to awaken our minds to the plight of others, these works are

DEDICATED TO YOU

My Sweet Little Star

I'm in space
with this sweet little star
held in my arms.
I snuggle
this sweet little star.
A cry that makes my tears chuckle
what a sweet little star.

I fell in love with the rhythm
of this sweet little star
that breathes life throughout the shape
of this sweet little star.

In pleasure, I retrieved this sweet little star
with eyes that twinkle.

Oh, my sweet little star.

A Mothers' Letter

Every year there's a Mothers Day.
Everyday you dedicate it to me.
When you scream Mom with excitement,
when you scream Mom with a tear,
when you scream Mom
because you just know
with those three letters,
I'll be there.

And Oh,
I feel the rush
when I hear those three letters there
because those three letters
brought me my best years.

Yes, every year brings A Mother's Day
and I'm happy you celebrate it with me.
But what I love the most is
you dedicate it to me.

Why Must They Bully Me

Why must they bully me?
Do I not have the right clothes?
Does my hair not look like yours?
I can't be your mirror image,
that, will hinder my growth.
Why must they bully me?
Am I not the latest trend?
Am I big or quite too thin?

Why must they bully me?
I didn't conform to a statistic
even though I shadow it.
Is it because I'm not so insecure
about my sinful flesh?

Why must they bully me?
Is there something that they see
in me, that they can't be?
Have I magnified their inadequacies?

I know why they bully me.
They have the tools to cut my tree
but not the life inside of me.

I know why they bully me.
Because I see greater
and my best days will always
walk in front of me...
that's why they bully me.

Dear Mother

Dear Mother,
When I think of you,
I think of strength
I think of love.
My dear Mother,
you're the perfect gift from above.
You are a soldier;
and Mother,
I'll be with you
just like your hearts beat.
Like you are for me.
Oh Mother,
your beauty is fresh wind in summer.
My sweet Mother,
I love you.

To My Mom Sharon

My Grandmother's Prayer

I don't know the days
you cried out on praying knees
or the days you thanked God
in advance for the change.
All I know is the day
I was pulled unexpectedly
the day I couldn't let go
the same day He grabbed me.
What would I do without you?
More so, your prayer.
Just to know you bound the spirit
that tempted me
in warfare.
I love you, and thank you
for being grand.
Thank you for your prayer
that pushed me into His plan.

For Gramommy
Caroline

His Resources

I see those hands reaching out to me
but those aren't mine to grab.
King is not my name,
and no the throne is not mine.

It is He who is within me.
that has touched you this way.
You can thank me on my gift.
and I will return the thanks to Him.

It's the route He chose for me.
I'm not worth a bending knee.
I'm just His child
with success branching
from different areas
of my tree.

For Pastor Dexter

A Soul's Honor

She's beautiful like Spring
You can't miss her unless she leaves.

Her smile is so contagious
a proverbs woman, an inspiration
and that's ok if I'm her servant
following in second place
like Elisha with Elijah
I'm able for more or same like grace.

She speaks words of wisdom
has a gift of discernment
She doesn't act without a plan
and once its made, she's determined.

Sent like sunshine,
she helps assist my decision.

What a privilege to connect
to the fire that's within her.

Oh how it warms my heart
just to be called her daughter.

I've been blessed.
She's a gift to my soul
from God our Father

For Lady Leisa

True Awe

I listened to the elder sing
with a voice so sweet and so strong.
Her hands lifted.
Her singing sung me right out of my chair.
I stood up right next to her
and she kept her hands lifted.

She knocked me a few times.
And no, I wasn't offended.
In her eyes, I wasn't there.

Have you heard an elder sing?
A voice so sweet and so strong.
Bumped me a few times
but I admire her true awe.
She loved Jesus so much,
nothing could hinder her song.

When I heard the elder sing, I tuned in.
Sounded like she was singing for her
and the next generations.

When I heard the elder sing,
I saw her singing above everything
trying to hinder her praise.

Mother, I respect your true awe.
This is your salute;
'Keep singing along'
I just love when I hear
an elder sing.

I'll Remember

I'll remember you
like I would a promise,
like I would a victory.
You're a special memory.
I'll remember
the care in your voice,
the compassion in your eyes,
your hand on my back.
Like my mother at my side
I'll always remember you,
Please remember me.

Thank you

For Mrs. Temple

Blended

You picked up your life
and set it in a new position
and for that
you're amazing.
And for that
I want to thank you.

You took a step
That's new to you
and told me
it was an honor.
And for that
I love you more.
You are the one
that I adore.
You took our hands
and made a commitment.
Since then
we became blended
and never ending.

My Little Red Person

I try to hide my little red person
when she burns it makes me boil.

I used to give her light now she's spoiled.

Gave her control
cause I was too weak to ignore her.

Why must the devil test my patience
while I try to keep her hidden.

Is it really the enemy?
Or are you attacking my little red person?

To make me better?
To develop strength.
To make me comfortable without her.
To strengthen my weaknesses.
To make my life pleasing.

Look!
here they come again, smirkin'.
They're coming to see
my little red person.

I don't understand.
When did she become
these tourists' attraction?

Look!
Here they come again, smirkin'.
But I won't let them see my little red person.

The Middle

This woman has raised
and wiped my tears for me.

If she bends,
she's bending backwards
and mostly because of me.

But to you,
She lies, the full story is never told.
She kept us hidden.
She's a riddle, it's too late to be civil

This man is just perfect for me.
My best friend,
my prayer partner.
He is the sight of fun.

He makes me laugh a laugh
that squeezes the
air from my lungs.
But to you, he's a liar too
and everything is about him.
I raised you by myself
He has no reason bustin' in
Don't forget me.
Don't forget our struggle
I love you both
I don't love anyone more.

Disagreements
You are my enemy
And you won't take away the best of me.

"Hi,"
'Middle' is what they call me.

The one that shouts
and no one hears.

Because I'm always listening.

Spirit vs. Body

This pain maybe incredible,
but body don't go against me.
His Spirit is in me,
so you must fight with me.

I will live
I will not die
My Lord, You need me here.

Before birth,
You instilled purpose
and I know *this* isn't it.
So body, heal and don't fall victim.

Time, you must be restarted.
Voice, draw my days back to me.
Mouth, speak life inside me more.
Ear, if you caught something different
then forget what you've heard.

I'm speaking life into my body.
It shall line up with the word.
I Am Alive.

His Healing Power

Spirit you have His healing power
Take over this weakling
and reach out to life for me.

Family don't cry over me.
I know I am amazing.
Don't think you have to save my memories.
I'm here to tell you
that's not what's left of me.

Life and death is on my tongue
and I still have it now to speak.
Thoughts line up and talk to me
and tell me I will live through this.
That'll give my heart a sweet kiss.

I cancel all things that will leave my spirit sour.
Hear me when I say it,
I carry His healing power.

Flesh To Sleep

Don't cry over me.
It's time for me
to put my flesh to sleep.

I knew I'd burst one day
with all of His power inside of me.

My spirit overrode my flesh so much
it couldn't handle me.

I admit when I was here
I've made some memories.

Don't live in sin.

Love like He said
and you will see me again.

www.ingramcontent.com/pod-product-compliance
Lightning Source LLC
Chambersburg PA
CBHW052358060726
47592CB00019B/1528

* 9 7 8 0 6 9 2 9 4 4 1 3 4 *